**discover** **countries**

# Discover Germany

## Camilla de la Bédoyère

**PowerKiDS**
press.

New York

Published in 2010 by The Rosen Publishing Group Inc.
29 East 21st Street, New York, NY 10010

First Edition

Concept design: Jason Billin
Editor: Susan Crean
Designer: Clare Nicholas
Consultant: Rob Bowden

Library of Congress Cataloging-in-Publication Data

De la Bédoyère, Camilla.
  Discover Germany / Camilla De la Bedoyere.
     p. cm. --  (Discover countries)
  Includes index.
  ISBN 978-1-61532-287-9 (library binding)
  ISBN 978-1-61532-292-3 (paperback)
  ISBN 978-1-61532-293-0 (6-pack)
  1.  Germany--Juvenile literature.  I. Title.
  DD17.D374 2010
  943--dc22

                         2009023732

Photographs:
1, Corbis/Reuters/Christian Charisius; 3, Corbis/dpa/Patrick Pleul (top), Konstantin Mironov (bottom); 4 (map), Stefan Chabluk; 5, Shutterstock/Kamil Sobócki; 6, Shutterstock/Kristin Speed; 7, Shutterstock/ultimathule; 8, Corbis/Reuters/Fabrizio Bensch; 9, Corbis/dpa/Tobias Felber; 10, iStock/Matthew Dixon; 11, Shutterstock/Konstantin Mironov; 12, Corbis/zefa/Uli Wiesmeier; 13, Corbis/dpa/Juergen Effner; 14, Corbis/Reuters/Christian Charisius; 15, Corbis/dpa/Patrick Pleul; 16, Corbis/dpa/Bernd Wuestneck; 18, Shutterstock/Luchschen; 19, Corbis/Reuters/Christian Charisius; 20, Shutterstock/Sascha Burkard; 21, Shutterstock/Govert Nieuwland; 22, iStock/Olga Shelego; 23, iStock/Jon Helgason; 24, Shutterstock/Holger Mette; 25, Corbis/Brooks Kraft; 26, Corbis/Bandphoto /Starstock/Photoshot; 27, Shutterstock/Henrik Andersen; 28, Corbis/dpa/Franz-Peter Tschauner; 29, Shutterstock/W. Woyke.
Cover images: Shutterstock/Dan Breckwoldt (left), Shutterstock/Jonathan Larsen (right)

Manufactured in China
CPSIA Compliance Information: Batch #WAW0102PK: For Further Information
contact Rosen Publishing, New York, New York at 1-800-237-9932

# Contents

Discovering Germany     4

Landscape and climate     6

Population and health     8

Settlements and living     10

Family life     12

Religion and beliefs     14

Education and learning     16

Employment and economy     18

Industry and trade     20

Farming and food     22

Transportation and communications     24

Leisure and tourism     26

Environment and wildlife     28

Glossary     30

Topic web     31

Further Information, Web Sites,
   and Index     32

# Discovering Germany

Germany is a large country at the center of Europe. It is more than twice the size of the state of California and has the largest population in the European Union. Germany shares borders with nine other countries. It has one of the world's strongest economies, and it is highly respected around the globe for the quality of its engineering.

## A country is born

Germany was once a region of many individual cities and states that ruled themselves. Each area had its own customs, traditions, and laws. In 1871, they were united as a single nation. German people call their country Deutschland.

## A nation divided

Germany fought and lost in both World War I and World War II. In 1949, after World War II, the nation was divided into East Germany and West Germany.

**DID YOU KNOW?**
In 1961, East Germany built a wall across Berlin. It stopped people from moving to West Germany. The Berlin Wall was knocked down in 1989. Pieces of it are still sold as souvenirs.

East Germany was ruled as a communist state, and West Germany became a republic. The country was reunified in 1990, and became the Federal Republic of Germany.

## Germany today

Germany has the world's third-largest economy, and most Germans enjoy a high standard of living. The nation is divided into 16 states, each with its own elected government. Germany's central government is a federal republic and is led by the chancellor. The chancellor is elected every four years.

German people are known for their contributions to art, books, music, engineering, and philosophy. They have experienced centuries of turmoil and war, but today live in a peaceful nation.

**Germany Statistics**

**Area:** 137,846 sq. miles (357,021 sq. km)

**Capital city:** Berlin

**Government type:** Federal republic

**Bordering countries:** Austria, Belgium, Czech Republic, Denmark, France, Luxembourg, Netherlands, Poland, Switzerland

**Currency:** Euro (€)

**Language:** German

Neuschwanstein Castle is a royal palace in the German region of Bavaria. It was built from 1869 to 1892.

# Landscape and climate

There are huge, snowy peaks, vast, green plains, and dense forests in Germany. The landscape is also shaped by farms and towns.

## Lowlands and highlands

Germany has three main regions: the plains, the uplands, and the highlands.

The highlands are located in southern Germany and include part of the Alps, Europe's largest mountain range. The spectacular Black Forest covers 2,320 sq miles (6,000 sq km) in the southwest highlands. Dense woodlands cloak the mountains, creating stunning scenery and making it a popular area with tourists. The River Danube begins in the Black Forest and flows eastward for 1,770 miles (2,850 km), reaching its mouth at the Black Sea. It is Europe's second-longest river, after the Volga.

The uplands of central Germany are high, flat-topped areas with steep sides, called plateaux. The uplands are known for their great beauty, with fast-flowing rivers, small mountains, and wild woods.

The northern plains make up half of the country. This region has been eroded by glaciers and rivers over thousands of years, creating large, sweeping, flat areas.

⚫ The green countryside and forests of Bavaria are overlooked by the Alps.

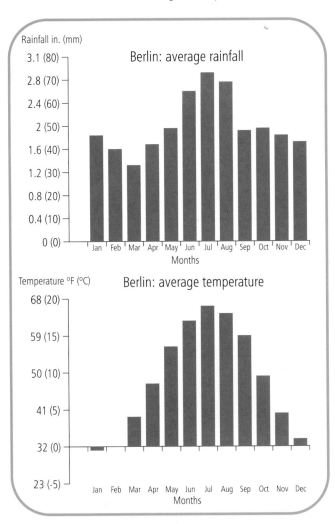

The soil is not very fertile, so much of the plains farmland is used for grazing cattle and sheep.

## The Rhine

The Rhine is Germany's most important river. It flows from the Alps northward. Industrial towns and ports were built along the Rhine, including Worms, Bonn, Cologne, and Düsseldorf. For centuries, people have traveled along the Rhine, trading their goods.

## Seasons of sun and snow

Germany has a temperate climate. It has four seasons and snow is common in the winter, especially in the mountainous highlands in the south. The plains benefit from mild winters and regular rainfall. This makes the north particularly suitable for farming.

▼ *The small town of Lorch is just one of many settlements that has developed along the banks of the River Rhine.*

### Facts at a glance

**Land area:** 134,836 sq. miles (349,223 sq. km)

**Water area:** 3,011 sq. miles (7,798 sq. km)

**Highest point:** Zugspitze 9,721 feet (2,963 m)

**Lowest point:** Neuendorf bei Wilster -11.5 feet (-3.5 m)

**Longest river:** Rhine River 865 miles (1,390 km)

**Coastline:** 1,484 miles (2,389 km)

**DID YOU KNOW?**

The Black Forest is famous for its wooden cuckoo clocks, which have been made in the area since the 1740s. The world's largest cuckoo clock is in the Black Forest town of Schonach.

# Population and health

Germany has a population of around 82 million. The population grew rapidly after World War II, but now it is falling. By 2050, Germany's population is expected to drop to 74 million.

Germans today are having fewer children than people did in the years following World War II. As a result, the German population is aging, and there are more Germans older than 65 than people younger than 15.

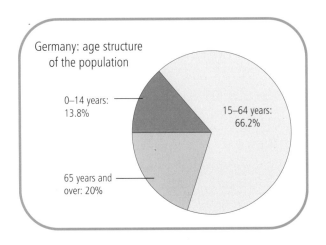

Germany: age structure of the population

0–14 years: 13.8%

15–64 years: 66.2%

65 years and over: 20%

## Migration

Recently, the German government and businesses invited foreign workers to come to Germany. This is because the falling population has meant there are fewer people who can work. From 1950 to 1955, about 55,000 people migrated into Germany. From 2000 to 2005, that figure jumped to 200,000.

In the 1960s, the government invited "guest workers" from Turkey to undertake unskilled jobs that no one else wanted. Many remained and set up their own communities. There are now around 2.5 million Turks living in Germany.

Turkish women walk in a street market in Berlin's Kreuzberg district, where many Turks live.

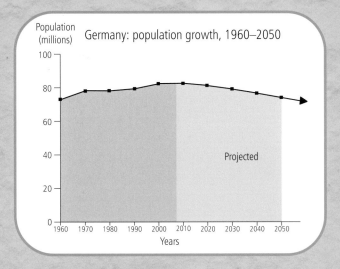

**Germany: population growth, 1960–2050**

Population (millions)

Projected

Years

## Healthy lives

A German born today can expect to live to about the age of 80. The German people benefit from good living conditions and a national healthcare system.

The main causes of death in Germany are heart and circulatory diseases. The next most common cause of death is cancer.

▶ Residents from a home for senior citizens enjoy an aqua gym fitness class.

**DID YOU KNOW?**
In 1901, a German scientist named Wilhelm Conrad Röntgen discovered X-rays. Doctors around the world use these invisible rays of light to detect and diagnose diseases.

## Facts at a glance

**Total population:** 82.4 million

**Life expectancy at birth:** 79.1 years

**Children dying before the age of five:** 0.4%

**Ethnic composition:** German 91.5%, Turkish 2.4%, other 6.1% (mostly made up of Greek, Italian, Russian, Serbo-Croatian, Polish, Spanish)

# Settlements and living

Around 75 percent of Germany's population lives in towns or cities, rather than rural areas. This is mainly due to Germany's industrial past, during which people moved from rural areas to towns and cities to find work.

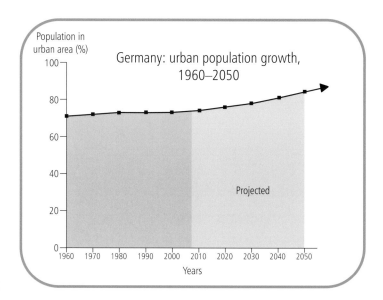

Germany: urban population growth, 1960–2050

Population in urban area (%)

Projected

Years

## Urban life

Cities provide Germans with better access to jobs, stores, schools, and entertainment than rural areas. They also have better facilities such as hospitals and transportation systems.

## Cities

Germany's capital city is Berlin. Before reunification, there were two capitals: Bonn in West Germany and East Berlin in East Germany. Large parts of Berlin were destroyed in World War II, but it has since been rebuilt. The city has a population of around 3.4 million people, and it is an important place for business and cultural activities.

Old and new buildings are found side by side in Berlin. The church on the right was damaged in World War II.

Other large cities in Germany are Hamburg, Munich, Cologne, and Frankfurt. Between them, they accommodate around 4.6 million people.

## Where people live

Most Germans rent their homes, which may be apartments or houses. Forty percent of people own their own home. However, people in eastern Germany are more likely to live in rural areas and rent their homes than people in western Germany.

Many small towns can be found throughout Germany. They often contain old buildings built in a traditional style. Heidelberg, for example, is an historic town near the River Rhine that dates back to the twelfth century. Every year, it attracts around 3.5 million visitors who come to see its old buildings. These include Germany's oldest university, the University of Heidelberg, which was founded in the fourteenth century.

**DID YOU KNOW?**
German place names give clues about an area. Towns near mountains may have "berg" at the end of their name, e.g. Gutenberg, which means "good mountain." A village name often ends in "dorf"—the word for a small settlement.

### Facts at a glance

**Urban population:** 73% (60.6 million)

**Rural population:** 27% (22 million)

**Population of largest city:** 3.4 million (Berlin)

▼ Heidelberg is popular with tourists, who like to visit the Old Town district of shops, winding roads, and historic houses.

# Family life

In Germany, as in many other European countries, family life has changed greatly in recent years. More women work outside the home than ever before, and couples have fewer children than in the past.

## Looking after the family

Most German children have parents who both work outside the home. Children help out around the home and are responsible for getting themselves ready for school.

Older members of the family are sometimes cared for at home, although Germany has a good welfare system. It provides care for people who need it, such as senior citizens and disabled people.

### Facts at a glance

**Average children per childbearing woman:**
1.4 children

**Average household size:**
2.1 people

▼ German families enjoy spending leisure time together. Here, a father and son canoe on a lake in Bavaria.

## Getting married

Marriage rates have fallen in Germany and unmarried couples often live together. Around 25 percent of all German children are born to parents who are not married. On average, people who do marry are between 25 and 30 years old. As the number of marriages has gone down, the number of divorces has gone up. Many German couples decide not to have children, and when they do, they are likely to have only one or two.

## Time together

The majority of German people believe that being part of a family helps them to be happy. Most young Germans say they have a good relationship with their parents, and 73 percent of all Germans from 18 to 21 still live at home.

▼ Senior citizens in Germany enjoy a high quality of life. Here, two German women sit on a bench in a meadow in Stuttgart.

# Religion and beliefs

Religious beliefs are important to most Germans, and research shows that almost half of them believe in God. Most Germans describe themselves as Christians. However, the number of Muslims and Jews in Germany has increased recently due to immigration.

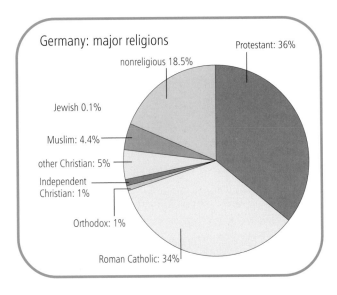

Germany: major religions

Protestant: 36%
nonreligious 18.5%
Jewish 0.1%
Muslim: 4.4%
other Christian: 5%
Independent Christian: 1%
Orthodox: 1%
Roman Catholic: 34%

## The Christian Church

Until about 500 years ago, most Europeans were Catholic. In 1517, a German priest, Martin Luther, wanted to reform, or change, the Catholic Church. He disapproved of the way some of the priests behaved and what they preached to their congregations.

Protestant Church Day was held in the German town of Hanover in 2005. Around 400,000 people attended.

Luther's actions led to a huge change in religious practice. The period became known as the Reformation and the Protestant, or Lutheran, Church was created. Protestantism spread through Europe—and beyond. Today, most Germans describe themselves as Christians and are either Catholic or Protestant. Less than 20 percent of them, however, go to church regularly.

## Festival time

The two most important festivals in Germany are the Christian festivals of Easter and Christmas. Celebrations also take place every year before Lent, the period that leads up to Easter, and people dress up to take part in street carnivals. These festive occasions are most common in Catholic parts of the country, especially the southern regions.

The first carnival in Cologne took place in the fourteenth century. Today, carnival-goers put on fancy costumes, paint their faces, and follow decorated floats as they parade through the town. People on the floats throw lollipops and candies into the crowd as they pass.

Christmas is eagerly anticipated by German children. Store windows are decorated to delight and entice passersby.

# Education and learning

German children start school when they are six, and most of them stay in education until they are 18 years old. Education and training are considered very important in Germany.

## Schools

Eighty percent of German children from three to six years old go to Kindergarten. After Kindergarten, children move up to *Grundschule*—primary or first school—until they are ten. From the ages of 10 to 15, Germans are educated at a *Hauptschule* (middle school). Most schools are open from 8 a.m. until lunchtime. Students then spend the afternoon doing homework or sports.

◀ Teenage students study German language in class.

## Learning to work

By the age of 15 or 16, German students are expected to have decided which type of career they would like. They choose their high school according to their talents and interests.

Some students, for example, might attend a *Berufsschule* (vocational school) where they take lessons and have on-the-job training for careers such as nursing, catering, and plumbing. Others attend *Realschule*, where they train to work in businesses such as banks, hotels, and stores. A *Gymnasium* is a school that educates students who are most likely to go to a university. These students aim for careers in professions such as medicine, accountancy, law, and teaching.

## Lifelong learning

The German government encourages adults to return to college to learn new skills. People who cannot find jobs because they are unskilled are given vouchers. These can be exchanged for training at local colleges and universities.

▼ Students who are learning to become bakers are shown how to make pastries and cookies.

# Employment and economy

Germany has Europe's biggest economy and is one of the world's most successful trading nations. Germany is successful because it exports more than it imports. In other words, it sells more goods than it buys—and this makes wealth.

## Where people work

Almost all working Germans are employed in industries and services. Industrial jobs include making goods in factories, such as cars and computers. Service jobs include working in stores, offices, or in public services such as transportation, health, and education. Today, less than 3 percent of all working Germans are employed in agriculture, forestry, and fishing.

Economic growth (%)

Germany: economic growth, 1980–2006

**DID YOU KNOW?**
Germany has one of the world's biggest economies. In 2007, the German economy earned $6.1 million every minute. That's more than $100,000 a second!

▼ The city of Frankfurt is one of Europe's most important financial centers. Many banks are located here.

## Unemployment

Germany has had a problem with unemployment since East and West Germany were reunified in 1990. Creating a new country involved joining different political and economic systems into one. Many people lost their jobs.

The German government gives unemployed people welfare benefits they can use to pay for food, housing, and other essential items while they look for work.

## Women at work

German unions are powerful, but they have not been able to help women to gain the same employment rights as men. On average, German women earn 22 percent less than men who do the same job. As in many other countries, German women are also less likely to hold senior jobs.

▶ Car manufacturing is important in Germany. An average of 550 new cars are collected from this giant car storage center in Wolfsburg, Germany, every day.

# Industry and trade

Germany is one of the world's leading exporters because it produces high-quality goods. Around one-third of all the goods that Germany sells abroad goes to France, the U.S., and the U.K.

## Secret of success

Many German factories employ experts in mechanical engineering to produce goods such as cars, ships, and machinery. Electrical engineers make products such as cell phones, televisions, and computers. The success of German manufacturing is partly due to the high skill level of German workers, who excel in design and technology.

Germany's position in the center of Europe has helped it become a successful trading nation. Germany has a good transportation system and its rivers, canals, roads, and railroads are used to carry goods to neighboring countries.

**DID YOU KNOW?** German electrical engineers wanted to improve sound quality on a telephone line. In 1987, they discovered a new way to store sound. It was the beginning of the MP3 format.

▼ Hundreds of containers are loaded onto a ship in a German port. From here, they can be transported worldwide.

## Raw materials

Substances that are used to make other goods are called raw materials. Germany has some raw materials, such as coal, salt, and potash (a fertilizer). However, it has to import most of the raw materials it needs for manufacturing. Iron is imported to make steel, and oil and gas are imported to provide energy.

Energy supplies, such as oil and gas, are expensive to import. German companies are researching better, cleaner ways to generate their own energy, such as hydroelectricity, solar power, and wind power.

## Coping with change

When West Germany and East Germany reunified in 1990, many businesses suffered, especially in the eastern region. Factories that made steel and textiles struggled to make money. Many of them closed down because they could not produce goods more cheaply than factories elsewhere in the world. Since then, German industries have had to concentrate on developing new products, especially computers and other electrical goods.

▲ Steel is produced at a large industrial center in Duisburg, on the River Rhine.

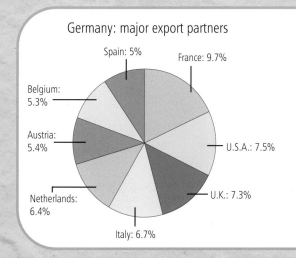

Germany: major export partners

Spain: 5%
France: 9.7%
Belgium: 5.3%
Austria: 5.4%
U.S.A.: 7.5%
Netherlands: 6.4%
U.K.: 7.3%
Italy: 6.7%

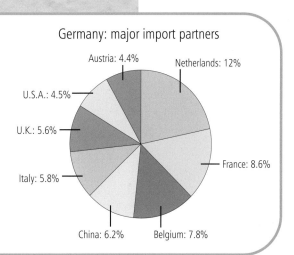

Germany: major import partners

Austria: 4.4%
Netherlands: 12%
U.S.A.: 4.5%
U.K.: 5.6%
France: 8.6%
Italy: 5.8%
China: 6.2%
Belgium: 7.8%

# Farming and food

Farming in Germany has changed since the 1980s, because many small farms have been merged to make bigger ones. Large farms are more productive, which means they can grow more food and make more money.

## On the farm

Most of Germany's agricultural land is used to grow cereals or as pasture for grazing animals. The most common crops are wheat, barley, corn, rye, and sugar beets. In addition, hops are grown to make beer, and grapes are grown to make wine. German farmers usually grow more food than is needed by their German customers, so the extra produce is sold to other countries.

### Facts at a glance

**Farmland:** 35% of total land area

**Main agricultural exports:** Cheese

**Main agricultural imports:** Livestock and crops, cheese, wine

**Average daily calorie intake:** 3,490 calories

▼ When harvested, these grapes will be used to make German wines.

## Forestry

Around one-third of Germany's land is covered with forests, and some of these are grown especially for the timber trade. Timber is wood that is used for making things, such as furniture and paper. Germany is one of Europe's largest producers—and users—of timber.

## A feast of flavors

Germany is a nation of regions, and each region has its own style of cooking. Pickled fish, for example, is popular in the north, meat loaf is popular in southern areas, and doughnuts are loved by Berliners. Some international foods originally came from Germany: hamburgers are named after the German town of Hamburg, and frankfurter sausages came from Frankfurt.

German specialities include sauerkraut (pickled cabbage), pumpernickel (rye bread), and bratwurst (sausages). Another speciality is apple strudel, a pastry made with apples, cinnamon, and raisins.

**DID YOU KNOW?**
Germany imports around 500,000 tons of cheese every year, but exports even more—around 700,000 tons. German cheese is sent to more than 60 countries worldwide.

▶ Traditional German sausages are served on a bed of sauerkraut. The German word for sausage is *wurst*.

# Transportation and communications

Germany has excellent transportation systems, including railroads, highways, and shipping. People and goods are able to move easily around and through the country. Many German transportation systems link up with those of neighboring countries, and this helps to make travel through Europe faster, safer, and cheaper.

## Roads and trains

After reunification, the railroads of West Germany and East Germany had to be modernized and a single railroad network, the Deutsche Bahn, was created. Around 350,000 people travel long distances by train every day, some of them on the Inter City Express trains, which can travel at up to 174 mph (280 kph).

### Facts at a glance

**Total roads:** 143,847 miles (231,500 km)

**Paved roads:** 143,847 miles (231,500 km)

**Railroads:** 29,959 miles (48,215 km)

**Major airports:** 66

**Major ports:** 8

▼ Inter City Express (ICE) trains were first developed in the 1980s. ICE trains run to Paris, Brussels, Zurich, and Amsterdam.

## Waterways

Germany has around 4,600 miles (7,500 km) of waterways, including rivers and canals. They carry around one-quarter of all Germany's freight.

The Rhine is one of Europe's most important waterways. It has been used to transportation goods for hundreds of years—even the Romans had a fleet of boats on the river. Parts of the Rhine have been straightened to make water transportation easier, and canals connect the river to German towns.

## Keeping in touch

Before reunification, East German telephone systems were poor, and it was not unusual for people to wait 12 years to get a phone installed. Since the 1990s, the German telephone system has been improved, to become one of the most advanced in the world.

In 2001, one-third of Germans used the Internet, but now it is available to two-thirds of the population—and that figure is growing. Cell phones are called Handys in Germany, and seven out of 10 people own one.

⬤ The city of Rostok lies where the river Warnow meets the Baltic Sea. It is an important shipyard and port.

### DID YOU KNOW?

An enormous, water-filled bridge connects two German canals. The Magdeburg Water Bridge is Europe's longest water bridge, at 570 miles (918 km). It was built from 24,000 tons of steel.

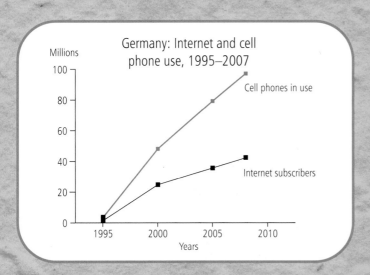

Germany: Internet and cell phone use, 1995–2007

Millions

Cell phones in use

Internet subscribers

Years

# Leisure and tourism

During their leisure time, Germans enjoy pastimes such as sports and traveling abroad. In addition, Germans spend time relaxing by visiting art museums, listening to music, and reading books.

## Country of culture

Germany has a rich cultural past. Beethoven, Bach, and Handel are three German-born composers whose music has been enjoyed for 300 years. Albrecht Dürer is regarded as one of Europe's greatest artists. He came from Nuremberg, and his paintings are on display in German art galleries. Karlheinz Stockhausen was born in Cologne in 1928. He became an important creator of modern classical music.

The Brothers Grimm lived in the 1800s and wrote fairy tales, such as Snow White and Rumpelstiltskin, which are still popular with many children today.

◀ The city of Berlin hosts open-air concerts.

## A sports-loving nation

Soccer is Germany's favorite sport, and people enjoy both watching it and playing it. The German soccer team has won the World Cup three times, and Germany hosted the World Cup in 1974 and 2006. Other popular sports include gymnastics, tennis, sailing, hiking, and cycling.

## Germany for tourists

Almost 20 million people traveled to Germany for vacations in 2007. Most of those visitors came from the Netherlands, the U.S., and the U.K. Tourists come to Germany to see sights such as historical towns and to visit stores and museums. Some of the most visited destinations include Berlin, the Black Forest, and the Bavarian Alps, where winter sports such as skiing and snowboarding are popular.

▽ Hiking through Germany's beautiful landscapes is a popular pastime.

### Facts at a glance

**Tourist arrivals (millions)**

| | |
|---|---|
| 1995 | 14.9 |
| 2000 | 19.0 |
| 2005 | 21.5 |
| 2006 | 23.6 |

### DID YOU KNOW?

Almost 80 percent of Germans vacation abroad every year. Most Germans take at least two vacations each year, usually in Germany or within Europe.

# Environment and wildlife

Sonder-glas

Germany is a developed country, and much of its natural habitat has been affected by building, farming, and industry. Like many other countries, Germany is now working to reduce the effects of these activities on the environment.

## Cleaning up

Rivers, land, and ocean waters have been contaminated by chemicals and other polluting materials. This problem is especially severe in the former East Germany. Burning coal to generate electricity caused acid rain, and some forests have been damaged by acid rain, particularly in southeast Germany and the Black Forest.

A number of chemical factories along the Rhine have been closed because of the chemical pollutants that they were releasing into the air and water. The German government now has strict rules about pollution, chemical safety, and waste disposal.

**DID YOU KNOW?**
Before 2002, the River Elbe was known as Europe's dirtiest river. After a long cleanup program, the Elbe was declared clean enough for swimming—and a party was held to celebrate in July 2002.

◯ At this glass recycling facility in Koblenz, used glass is sorted, melted, and processed so it can be turned into new glassware, such as bottles.

## Renewable energy

Germany is committed to reducing its contribution to global warming, which is partly caused by the burning of fossil fuels such as oil and coal. The government aims to reduce the nation's carbon emissions by 40 percent between 1990 and 2020 by using renewable energies, such as solar and wind power. Wind is Germany's most important renewable energy, and there are more wind turbines here than in any other country in the world. At the moment, wind turbines supply around 5 percent of all electricity in Germany.

## National parks

Germany has many National Parks where habitats such as forests and marshlands are protected. Harz National Park is home to a number of lynx. These big cats became extinct in the Harz Mountains more than a hundred years ago, but they have recently been reintroduced to the area.

▶ About 5 percent of Germany's energy needs are provided for by wind power.

# Glossary

**Catholic** largest branch of the Christian community, led by the Pope

**climate** normal weather conditions of an area

**communism** economic and political system in which all people are supposed to have an equal share of a nation's property and wealth

**communist state** form of government that operates under a system whereby all property is publicly owned

**contaminated** soiled, infected, or made dirty

**culture** way of life and traditions of a particular group of people

**economy** way that trade and money are controlled by a country

**eroded** worn away by wind, water, or ice

**export** good or service that is sold to another country

**federal republic** a government made up of states that are united by a central power

**fertile** good for growing crops, especially in large quantities

**GDP** total value of goods and services produced by a country

**glacier** large, slow-moving body of ice found on land

**habitat** the place, or type of place, where a plant or animal normally lives

**hydroelectricity** electricity that is generated using the power of falling or fast-moving water

**immigration** movement of people to a foreign country to live

**import** good or service that is bought from another country

**landscapes** physical features (such as mountains, rivers, and deserts) of a place

**manufacturing** making products, usually from raw materials

**migration** movement of people from one place to another

**philosophy** study of basic ideas about knowledge, right and wrong, truth, God, and the meaning of life

**pollution** substances that contaminate or poison, such as chemical waste

**republic** a system of government in which people elect officials to make decisions on their behalf

**reunified** brought a divided country together again

**rural** to do with the countryside or agriculture

**temperate climate** a mild climate that is neither extremely hot nor extremely cold

**textiles** fabric or cloth

**unemployment** being without paid work

**unions** organizations of workers who join together to protect their rights

**urban** to do with towns and town life

**welfare system** a system where the government takes responsibility for people's well-being, e.g., giving money to the unemployed, helping senior citizens and disabled people, and providing healthcare.

# Topic web

**Use this topic web to explore German themes in different areas of study.**

**History**
Find out what you can about communism. Which countries are no longer communist, and how many still have this political system in place?

**Geography**
Germany has areas of karst landscape. Find out what this means, and identify three other countries that have this feature.

**Science**
There are plans to reintroduce wolves to Germany. Why are some species of animal, such as lynxes and wolves, reintroduced to an area— and what problems might they cause?

**Math**
The German currency is the Euro (€), which is used in many other European countries. How much is €10 worth in U.S. dollars? Calculate the value of €5 and €100.

# Germany

**English**
Write a fairy tale in the style of the Brothers Grimm. Imagine your reader is a child from six to eight years old.

**Citizenship**
Germans are part of the European Union. Find out when this organization began and write a list of all of its current member nations.

**Design and Technology**
Explore the role German inventors Karl Benz and Gottlieb Daimler played in the invention of the car, and the contributions that modern German designers have made to the car industry.

**Information Technology**
Use the Internet to find some simple German recipes and make some simple German dishes, such as apple strudel, warm potato salad, or pretzels.

# Further Information, Web Sites, and Index

## Further reading

*Germany: The Culture* by Kathryn Lane (Crabtree Publishing Company, 2001)
*Letters From Around the World: Germany* by Cath Senker (Cherrytree Books, 2005)
*The European Union Today* by Simon Ponsford (Sea to Sea Publications, 2008)

## Web Sites

Due to the changing nature of Internet links, PowerKids Press has developed an online list of Web sites related to the subject of this book. This site is updated regularly. Please use this link to access this list:
http://www.powerkidslinks.com/discovc/germany/

## Index

acid rain 28
aging population 8
Alps 6, 27

Bavaria 5, 12, 27
Berlin 4, 6, 8, 10, 11, 27
Berlin Wall 4
Black Forest 6, 7, 27, 28
Bonn 7, 10
Brothers Grimm 26

canals 20, 25
car manufacturing 18, 19, 20
carnivals 15
cell phones 20, 25
chancellor 5
cheese 22, 23
children 8, 9, 12, 13, 15, 16, 17, 26
Christmas 15
Cologne 7, 11, 15, 26
composers 26
cuckoo clocks 7

Danube River 6
design and technology 20
Deutsche Bahn 24
Dürer, Albrecht 26
Düsseldorf 7

Easter 15
Elbe River 28
electrical goods 20, 21
energy 21, 29
engineering 4, 5, 20
exports 18, 20, 21, 22, 23

factories 18, 20, 21, 28
farming 7, 22, 28
Federal Republic of Germany 5
foreign workers 8
Frankfurt 11, 23

glaciers 6

Hamburg 11, 23
hamburgers 23
Harz National Park 29
heart disease 9
Heidelberg 11
highlands 6, 7
high standard of living 5, 9, 13
hops 22

imports 18, 21, 22, 23
Internet 25

jobs 8, 10, 17, 18, 19

*Kindergarten* 16

life expectancy 80
lynxes 29

Magdeburg Water Bridge 25
marriage 13
Martin Luther 14
MP3 20
Munich 11
museums 26, 27

plains 6, 7
pollution 28
ports 7, 20, 24

railroads 20, 24
Reformation 14
renting 11
reunification 5, 10, 19, 21, 24, 25
Rhine River 7, 11, 25, 28
roads 11, 20, 24

sauerkraut 23
schools 10, 12, 16, 17
senior citizens 9, 12, 13
soccer 27
Stockhausen, Karlheinz 26

timber 23
training vouchers 17
traveling abroad 26
Turks 8

unions 19
uplands 6

wealth 18
welfare system 12, 19
wind power 21, 29
wine 22
women's rights 19
World War II 4, 8, 10
Worms 7

X-rays 9